Hawthorne,
a House in Bolinas

a poem by

Ellen Sander

Finishing Line Press
Georgetown, Kentucky

Hawthorne, a House in Bolinas

Copyright © 2017 by Ellen Sander
ISBN 978-1-63534-172-0 First Edition
All rights reserved under International and Pan-American Copyright Conventions.
No part of this book may be reproduced in any manner whatsoever without written permission from the publisher, except in the case of brief quotations embodied in critical articles and reviews.

ACKNOWLEDGMENTS

To all those herein named, generously willing or unwitting mentors, and to the community of Bolinas, my love and thanks. My deepest appreciation to Joel Lipman, whose guidance and encouragement significantly evolved this work.

And, of course, thank you everyone at Finishing Line Press.

You Rock.

List of Illustrations

All photos by Ellen Sander

Page 5   Tom Clark at the dining table at Hawthorne
Page 6   Creeley House on Terrace Avenue
Page 11 Aram Saroyan and Gerard Malanga cavorting (from the collection of Gerard Malanga)
Page 14 Magda Cregg
Page 24 Duxbury Reef
Page 29 Fishing boats in the channel
Page 30 Bench on the riprap at the end of Wharf Road

Excerpt from "September" by Joanne Kyger reprinted with gracious permission of the poet

Publisher: Leah Maines
Editor: Christen Kincaid
Cover Art: Ellen Sander
Author Photo: Ellen Sander
Cover Design: Elizabeth Maines McCleavy

Printed in the USA on acid-free paper.
Order online: www.finishinglinepress.com
            also available on amazon.com

Author inquiries and mail orders:
Finishing Line Press
P. O. Box 1626
Georgetown, Kentucky 40324
U. S. A.

Bolinas memories 1971-1978, visitors to a wood house
in a north coastal village, the poets and the everpresent rumble
of the Pacific exhaling across the mesa

*For Marin Sander-Holzman, so bravely born, boldly grown.
And for Arthur Okamura, who adorned Bolinas with his art,
his wit and his love.*

The road to Bolinas bends
around estuaries where imperial
beziers of blue heron and
snowy egret repose standing

The Big Mesa rises from the beach, skirted
by sand cliffs, rolls to the Palomarin trailhead
where outspread seagulls
and osprey dive, red tail hawk soar
roads and grassland, cliffs and homes
paths and byways
overhung with cypress, eucalyptus, dense fog
and a murmuration of poets

〜〜
〜〜

Beneath mesas, a town of
dusty cafes, liquor store and a bar
bookstore, laundry, hardwares and surf shop

From the tin roof of the gas station
a lazing beagle oversees it all
the day I arrive:
This must be the place

Okamura on a ladder murals an outside wall
paints each monarch butterfly and quiffed wave

Postmistress Annie sang the
National Anthem each Independence Day
the entire town parties in the street

Up on the mesa, in a wood frame house on
Hawthorne, a strip of unpaved road
from Elm to the ocean cliff
firestove, sunwashed windows
(when there was sun)
kitchen busy with muffins and stew

Garden, wildflowers, woodpile
quiet brimming nights

not just nights entwined or conjoined but
time   when passions
graced
daylight, discourse

and traffic of infamy and brilliance
visiting the house on Hawthorne
between Tamalpais' foothills and the sea

∽

The first moon arrives, itself visited

the screen's full of a
footprint on the moon

Baby moves in my belly

∽

Paul Williams, spirit brother,
whose writing pulled me out of myself
whose friendship illuminated my life
writer and Crawdaddy publisher
comes to Bolinas to see his
godson into the world

A long
autumn night
chenille bedroom
labor sitter, friends, a young Buddhist monk
the whole room in rhythm and huffing with me

Paul plays Here Comes the Sun
as the end of night
opens through my body

Thankful to be in my own bed
cradling my treasure

A few days later punky mensch
Raymond Mungo comes by to gather Paul
and leave the next morning to board
a freighter for 11 days to Kobe where
Paul jilts Ray and meets Sachiko
who becomes his second wife

Ray journeys on to
Hong Kong, Bangkok
Malaysia and Nepal where
he finds a guru who tells him
go home
hence
Return to Sender

∼∼∼
∼∼∼

Nursing, a tremble of pleasure
with each little suck

4AM feedings with
the ocean's echo

against the mesa
the dark hush

peppered with birdcall
whitetail deer

strutting cliques of
pheasant and

Miwok spirits

∿

Almost every morning
Tom Clark comes by
five, six in the morning
even if it was dark
cutting across the narrow
footworn path from his
house on Nymph and Cherry
sometimes with
2 year old Juliet
her quiet gaze, long hair
rosebud mouth

He brings poetry, his latest book
or something found on the path
my infant and I
we never feel alone

Coffee, splendid conversations on
grey mornings, amazing to have
such neural simpatico
no need to talk
but for the river and the joy of it

In Green, he inscribes
"a piece of the same person"
It's been different, my person, ever since

∿∿
∿∿

In fogged up mornings, riots of
nasturtium and wild rose punctuate the
misty sheen on roadsides and paths

I walk Hawthorne to Ocean
Herman Berlandt, frowny forehead even
when he smiles, nods as we pass

Meandering down Terrace
a bowed slope toward town
dazzling clusters of Monarchs
drape eucalyptus limbs
in trembling banners

Inside the white porched Creeley
house in the curved nape of Terrace
always coffee and conversation waiting

Bobbie Louise Hawkins
unraveling yarns
of Texas and travail
delivered in dialects
crinkled smiles, hilarity
dark glinting eyes

The soul of crackling wisdom, she
gave her salty sense of self as deft
paintings at dinner parties

Blazed when amused
detonated when enraged
the full damn package

〰︎

Bolinas is festooned with young mothers
crimson ginger black striped
blankets bulging with babies
backpacks and frontpacks of babies

Ocean Lee, Ben, Marin,
Felicidad, Pavati, Ian, Alishani and Kai
array the road that horseshoes
through town from
the Brighton to
the Wharf beach

in the shimmer of
the lifting mist

〰︎

Phoebe MacAdams as dazzling a beauty
who ever walked
seaside roads in wafts of fog, she
cradling Ocean in a velvety blanket
shawls tracing ripples around her
poems coalescing in her air

〰️

12 noon
Smiley's Schooner Saloon just opened

Bob Creeley, drinking alone
Sidelong dust filings drift
on a shaft of light
from an upper window, fall on
cigarette burns like black fingers on
the bar's polished lip

Bob has a shot with a beer back
flicks a finger at the bartender
points to me, I
get Irish coffee with Bushmills

We hover the drinks
with a reciprocity of quiet grunts

He's sheepish after
trying to make long distance calls
on my kitchen phone
when he and one of
my boyfriends
stagger in one sotted night
after closing time
I'm in bed pushing the switchook
to disconnect them

Creeley palms his
blue and orange crocheted hat
circling it around, plops
it on my head crooked

I fix it in the mirror with
a big cheese smile
He laughs so hard I think
he'll keel the barstool

I love it when men send me money
Wintering in Buffalo
Creeley sent a reply to my letter enclosing
a McGraw Hill royalty check
for $1.38 and wrote
on the back *for sweet Ellen Sander but
only in the bar*

He didn't sign it
I didn't cash it
I still have it,
framed, and have
as well, that hat

Aram Saroyan,
his gangly grace of perpetual
adolescence, drops by
often and sometimes with
Strawberry and Cream and Gaylen
and one day with Gerard Malanga
who says call me Ace, is that all right?

O My Generation on the
cherrywood table with the
lupine and the glass, the
wine and the sourdough, the
books and the baby seat
overlooking a tousled yard

Writers in velvet chairs, unbraid
we jam verbose
Bitches Brew, Peet's Arabica
Blue Heron croissants, smoke and
the brume of the mesa

One bougainvillea afternoon
Aram appears and slinks like a sack into a chair
dejected because his dad told him to forget about
this poetry stuff and get a real job writing short fiction

Down Elm Road toward Agate Beach
sits the orderly barnish Bolinas
Community Public Utility District
building Bobos call the beepud

Readings, concerts
parties, dances, town meetings and
weddings fill after hours
evenings and festive weekends

The water board is the town polity, reborn
after a Standard Oil tanker
slimes Bo Beach in January 1971
Enviro-activists converge
shampooing birds, rescuing seals
making headlines

Enviro-hippies take over the water board
Once they finish building their homes
they ordinance a halt to all new construction
Bo goes smug and small into the 21st century
infuriating developers, who sue and lose

The BPUD is the site of annual Harvest Balls
after growers reap their bounty
The Duxbury Reefers play
carpenters and poets dance
bud flows like beer

The first Bolinas Women's Dinner
comes to pass at the BPUD

Potluck of our finest fare
beets with barley, corn bread, chicken

Salad of mustard flower, freesia, borage and
nasturtium blossoms that grow wild

from the mesas, rosewater rice
carrot cake, a Grand Marnier whiff

in the cream cheese frosting
Wine, poems, handmade music

a raid of bellydancers
get us on our feet, zaghareeting

We love being women in Bolinas

∿
∿

Magda holds overnight
women's peyote circles
on a secluded beach

When invited, I decline
I can't do an overnight
I have a baby at home

Mary Coleman promptly says
my daughter Bethany will babysit
You're coming

Landlocked by the full moon high tide
we sing and chant all night
laugh 'til we weep
drink peyote tea brewed on the fire
hike out in the morning

Piney mulch bouquet of
eucalyptus and the Pacific
infuse the cool dawn

〰〰

October day '74, sunny, in shreddy clothes, working on my detached writing studio, desk, skylights, shelves, cocoon. ..phone.rings..   Bob Dylan says he's calling from the BPUD pay phone. Preschool and Hearsay News production hubbub, plenty hubbub at the BPUD nobody notices Bob Dylan.
Comes by Hawthorne a Bo break from Blood on the Tracks no whistle no warning, brown corduroy, spies the mandolin asks me play some, yes & as well my sound of the sea dulcimer song, he pats the table musing   I finally up the guts & ask so? you got one?
His slow grin could've
lit the Grand Canyon.
Sings the album through. Lilly, Rosemary and the Jack of Hearts lasts over 10 minutes at my kitchen table ~ when he closes his eyes, hits that reedy legato *blue* in Tangled I quietly explode   shadows shift softly up the walls I demo two finger chords he tries my mandolin, I see him oh I want one, send him to see Peter Rowan's mandolin collection He admires a hazy photo of Leonard Cohen his way out the door I think he thought it was him

∼∼
∼∼

Just before sunset Allen Ginsberg arrives
not to see me but
to gather a visiting blond young son of a
prominent public television family for love

We sit
the dusk, the windsound
the fragrance of tea
Allen teaches me to meditate
in 10 seconds:

> Just feel the breath as it
> goes in, see—and out
> your nostrils, breathe
> in breathe
> out and
> just notice
> about the breathing that's all

that's all
Yes, all
I got it
I get it

My world radiates in waves from this simple visit

> (
> Eons later I learn that this is the only
> technique that the Buddha taught
> this breath
> and feeling breath
> just breath
> life depends on it
>)

He spends the night
Allen Ginsberg fucked here
I'm up early enough to see him
lumber down the porch stairs

I wish he'd stayed for breakfast

〰️

on Christmas Eve Ramblin' Jack Elliott
shows up to drink   with Jim Roberts
hang and drink   with Jim Roberts
talk and drink   with Jim Roberts
jam and drink
and drink and drink
before leaving for Texas to see his daughter

My live-in love for a time, Jimmy, an
intermittent drunk and a lyricist
had some outstanding drinking buddies

Jack was already drunk when he got here
he visits a while, then
starts his juddery car
and aims it toward Texas

He loved that daughter so much
nothing could keep him
from going to Texas
to be with her for Christmas
even if he was going to be a little late

That alone can keep a man alive
in enemy territory

Jimmy nosedived into a cheating binge
planking any twat who'd return his smile
flaunting inland hippie girls in the bar and
throwing it in my face

I kicked his unsorry ass out of Hawthorne
with one of those caterwauling infidelity brawls not
unknown or even uncommon in Bolinas

Peter and Leslie Rowan came by to
see me through the aftermath
Peter with songs of comfort
let me play his mandocello which drones
in my sinew to this day

I have rarely known so fine a love as Peter's
we who were never lovers

(but, as it turns out, get this,
Jimmy and Leslie were)

On Joanne Kyger's 40th birthday
I bring an amanita mushroom
from a eucalyptus grove by Elm after a rain

I carry it like a wedding bouquet
two-step into her kitchen and we
make an omelet
glimmer all the afternoon

Arthur Okamura comes by with gifts, himself a gift
Arthur reflects on his art class
"I teach them, loosen the death grip
on the brush and let it move"

That night Joanne gives
a reading at the BPUD
it's packed, she
refers to herself as Joanne Elizabeth Kyger
before reading September :

>   *Well I myself am not myself*
>
>   *and which power of survival I speak*
>   *for is not made of houses.*
>
>   *It is inner luxury, of golden figures*
>   *that breathe like mountains do*
>   *and whose skin is made dusky by stars.*

Her regal stance flowing
hair and jacket, long skirt flowing
husky pliant voice
pulling the room into a radial center

〰︎
〰︎

Richard Brautigan accuses me
of being too famous when we met

He never makes it to Hawthorne
like he said he would
at Margot Doss' dinner party

When he inexplicably takes his life
he isn't found for days, for which
Rolling Stone pillories Bolinas

We're stunned
We never got to know him

♒

Lewis MacAdams
black armband
head bowed
walks the steep road up
Mt. Tam
for Jack Boyce's funeral

I stop the car
to pick him up
he says

>   I
>   have to
>   walk

I learn something
of human bond and
how it melts

Buddhist funeral chant
no body, no attachment, no joy, no grief

Peter Weston, Amy Niman, baby Jonah Coleman and David Sorrels
all die during those years

〰︎

Diane Gardiner brings
Lovely, fine-boned
sweet-needy Pamela Courson
to the shelter of Hawthorne
when she couldn't face L.A.
after Jim Morrison dies in Paris

deferring sorrow, almost
I half believe Jim
is secretly alive

until I see her
beautiful face
crushed to gravel

We hug and weep
like coyotes, like crows

Knuckles so cold
ripping winds bleed them

Jacket balloons, crackles
at the torn rim of the bluff
over Duxbury reef

Nudibranchs blush
anemone squirt
in minus-tide
tidepools

Sand and shale
sliver down the cliff wall
soft clicking shiver streams
falling
    all day
    all day
    all night
    all night
tick-ticking

〜

Paul Krassner is having a nervous breakdown
visiting Alan Watts in Muir woods

I hear this finding out
he's not coming to Hawthorne
It's all I can manage, he says
to hang on to the edge
so I drive over
to Roger Somers' compound

Sculpted redwoods, stone walks
trees at arabesque
curvilinear structures
bathrooms open
to the cragged ocean

I confide what I know
that letting go
hitting bedrock
is less painful
than clutching the edge

Distraught as he is
the gleam of
his astonishing intellect
quivers cross his face

Years later he has the nerve to call me
the Zelig of the revolution
when a picture of me bursting into tears as
Eldridge Cleaver bare handed dirt
into Jerry Rubin's grave
appeared with the obit in the L.A. Times

To set the record straight
I was crying for Eldridge, not Jerry

Adrienne and Neil Anderson
bring Jerry and Stella with them
from Mill Valley
When they leave
Jerry stays behind

He is seething in
spasms of jealousy
shame and fury

I kept pouring, finally
he said, he understood
alcohol, it dulls
feelings
pot intensifies

∿∿

Joanna Harcourt-Smith
calls herself Joanna Leary
glib-libs her way in the door
hits up all my friends for money
Her hustle is she's getting
Timothy out of prison

She borrows my most beautiful dress
(I have some trouble getting it back)

Denim and long with orchids embroidered
it's handmade by Susanna who I met when
she was married to Neil Young
and her name was Susan

Susan created the back cover
After The Gold Rush
patches on his jeans
she who is Cinnamon Girl
she who is the *you* in
I'm going to give you
Till the Morning Comes
One haughty mirthful beauty of a
redhead dame, we did a lot
of wine and laughing

∿

Susanna and I liberated
the pool table at Smiley's
No women cued up at that puny
bar-sized put-up-a-quarter table
so uneven half your expertise lay
in knowing where the gullies were

Which is not to say we could really play
but we dressed to compensate and
like to think we decorated
the only game in town
well enough to cover until we learned
to hold the table for a few games

Creeley didn't even play pool, so what was his beef?
After I missed a chump shot some hazy night
around Thanksgiving 73 he walked over
and growled
you need glasses!

≈

One night the power goes down in Bolinas
Smiley's goes dark, the jukebox silent
a kerosene lantern arrives
and the pool game continues

Ed Tinker, a handyman
red beard and herringbone pub cap
brings his guitar
Perry Fly comes in with his fiddle
and there is music

≈

Steely sea green morning fog
sitting on the Blue Heron bakery stoop
cinnamon bun still warm

American Spirit smoke curls round
my double shot Bobo Latte
the porch fills up

〰️

Out Wharf Road
small boats whisper in the restive channel
sea lions poke out of the water

Josh Churchman brings his boat in
ties her up
hands me a halibut
on his way to the store

〰️

I'm reading letters
on the bench perched
on the riprap overlooking the channel
watching tufts of fog escape from the brush
on mounded blonde foothills

Ephemeral light on days like this
whitecaps haiku the ocean

〰️

Driving home from over the hill one
moist grey day, I bank a
downhill curve on Shoreline Highway
The fog-filtered light ricochets off
wet road that
turns for an instant
to luminous silver ribbon

〰️

Jann Wenner looks me up when he and Janie
are searching for a house in Marin
checking out Bolinas

The contractor's wife wouldn't let the
realtor show the house because the realtor had
slept with her husband

They come by Hawthorne flabbergasted
It isn't far into the seventies, but
the sixties are over, for sure

≈

Tampering the election, Nixon
slinks out like a skunk when he gets caught

Gene Schoenfeld aka Dr. Hip
and John Grissom
come over from Stinson, hunch
over coffee at the butcher block table
gloating, interrupting
bitch slapping the Chronicle

I liked to tell the story of two 3 year old boys
bareback on a pony named Dusty I'm leading
while they have a conversation about God

My son says "I think God is like your father
and he is everywhere"

Benjamin says "Don't be stupid. God
is in Heaven. My father lives in Stinson Beach."

By "my father," Benjamin meant Gene

Gene calls the next day and rebukes me
in a quiet, halting sentence for
calling Benjamin his son in front of people

Ben's mother wasn't sure if Ben was Gene's
or not, but you just look
at that little munch and you know instantly
I had no idea Gene didn't know

Gene, Benjamin has to be yours
your miniature in every way
the cocky way he walks
the snoozy way he loves, his monkey wisdom

Gene sobs over the phone
has Ben over the next day
and eventually takes him in
Those two guys
looking after one another for years

≈

Jerry Wexler and an entourage of
San Francisco writers
come out to Hawthorne one Sunday
the limousine bouncing along the
not-a-county-maintained road

We sit in the yard among the
agathea cape daisy, the
garter snakes, brioche, apricot jam
steaming pots of tea and java

In my former life as a rock and roll hooligan
Jerry introduced me to Phil Spector at a
Crosby Stills and Nash recording session
at Heiders in L.A., as "a fine writer"
Spector squinted me down
"that comes from the right place"

Jerry is concerned that I
have to do all those dishes
after they leave—it's not a problem

I'm content washing dishes
in the solitary rustic twilight
the wind's brushy pass across the mesa
the cedars' throaty rustle

〰〰

Woodsmoke lifts from chimneys
a coiled diaphanous dance

Nighttime cool brushes my lips
in the yard, craning back
to take in the upside down
bowl of night sky's flinty swarms of stars

In a blazing streak of death agony
one singles me out

The elegance of expression
the proximal rhythm
life and death, day to day
the beauty of ordinary moments
with extraordinary beings
good company, belly laughs and hot tubs
in the chill north coast air

where the difference between
dense fog and light rain
is strictly semantic

Ellen Sander, a pioneering New York rock journalist, author of *Trips: Rock Life in the Sixties*, incubated her poetry in Bolinas, California in the seventies. Hawthorne is her homage to those poets and those times in Bolinas, in the early mid 1970's when Bolinas was rife with poets and poetry, in a thriving and spicy small town culture. After a stint in Los Angeles, she was an editor at *Women of China* magazine in Beijing in 2005, having taught college Conversational English in both Xiamen and Beijing. She was the Poet Laureate of Belfast, Maine in 2013 and 2014, where she lives today, near Head of the Tides. Her poetry has been published in *Chiron Review, Social Anarchism, Saturday Afternoon Journal, Dongxi, The Maine Review, Fredericksburg Literary and Art Review, Off The Coast,* the 2016 anthology, *Cross-Strokes* as well as the relaunch of *Oculus Vox*. She is on the board of the Belfast Poetry Festival and a member of Beyond Baroque.

Her son, daughter-in-law, grandchild live in Brooklyn, New York, her siblings in Manhattan so regular forays to the Empire City are a recurring itinerary.